LET WORDS LIKE SUNBEAMS WARM YOUR HEART

SHAFTS
OF LIGHT

KAYE HOLLINGS

Ark House Press
PO Box 1722, Port Orchard, WA 98366 USA
PO Box 1321, Mona Vale NSW 1660 Australia
PO Box 318 334, West Harbour, Auckland 0661 New Zealand
arkhousepress.com

Cataloguing in Publication Data:
Title: Shafts of Light
ISBN: 978-0-6450153-4-8 (hdbk.)
Subjects: Poetry; Photography; Christian Living;
Other Authors/Contributors: Hollings, Kaye

Design and layout by initiateagency.com

To all those who have
observed
imagined
pondered
and felt
the rhythms of life
with the
ups
and
downs
of being human
and who have reached out
through beauty
and bruises
to touch
the presence of God

CONTENTS

CONTENTS

From The Author

Join me on this reflective journey as I introduce you to wonderful people I've met and amazing places I've been as they reveal both the joys and struggles of life.

I have always loved reading poetry and have also been writing it for a long time. This book is a compilation of my poems written over many years and published now as a legacy of love for my family and friends.

I would like to thank my husband Cliff for all his support over the last 47 years, for being a steady influence when my wild ideas could have led me astray, and mostly for his love and his affirmation of my writing.

I hope that all who read *Shafts of Light* will be heartened and refreshed in new and positive ways.

WRITTEN AFTER A TIME
OF MULTIPLE LOSSES
WHEN I THOUGHT ALL
STRENGTH HAD GONE

FLY

Flapping in puddles in panic
from this level life is tough
Lord, lift my aching heart
give me courage and new start
help me rise above the muck

Soaring on high like an eagle
familiar nest lost to view
Lord catch me when I fall
send updraughts when I stall
help me fly, not flap with You

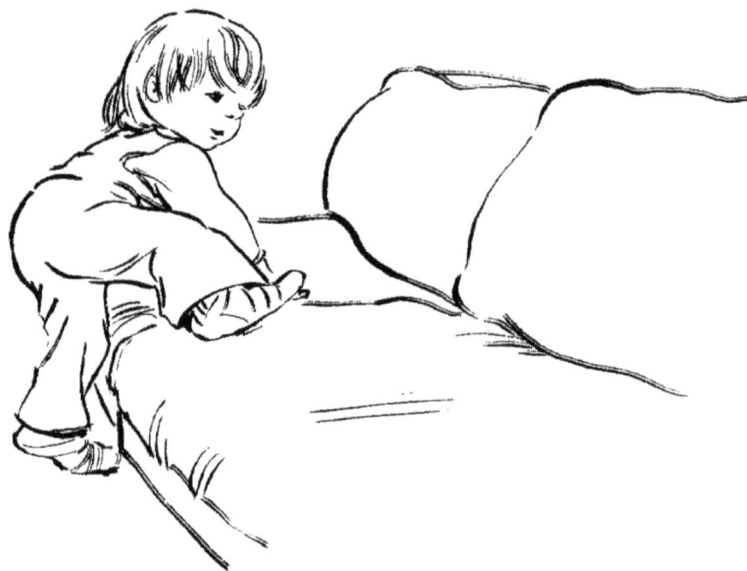

Love Is

To wipe the tears of naughtiness
to blow that running nose
to kiss those grubby, chubby cheeks
to scrub the neck just so
to adjust pyjama buttoning
to fix wrongly put-on shoes
to repair those grazed and bleeding knees
to praise even when they lose
to pretend it is a big surprise
to enjoy a tuneless song
to tell that story over again
to admit that you are wrong -
Is to love a child

First published 1983 in Fortesque and Friends,
an illustrated volume of children's poems, my first book, now out of print

His Music

Edvard Grieg's composing cabin overlooking a spectacular fjord in Bergen, Norway. Nature and music remain a magic combination

Green of leaf
blue of sky
smell of grass
and
fresh-turned sod
speak audibly of God

Smile of sun
caress of wind
kiss of rain
and
star-shaped flakes
His autograph make

Blind of eye
deaf of ear
he not attuned
to
soul's music
is less a man

CAGED

He sits immobile with a sad, grey face
alive yet trance-like and fixed
eyes that are glazed
ears permanently dazed
mind shut down, thoughts mixed

She chatters on, endless words hit the walls
laughing, crying, so confused so trapped
body that won't rest
always stressed
between her and reality huge gap

The caged bird wears many masks
hiding hurt and pain that can kill
locked in with strife
locked out from life
in the world of the mentally ill

I have no key to unlock the cage
but can pass friendship and love through the bars
to hold a hand
with family stand
seeing aching heart not deep scars

Parched Hearts

The unique, challenging beauty
of the Australian outback
leaves its imprint

Desert dawn climbs wearily
over landscape with skin peeled back
red, raw, hurting
life aborting
country panting for breath

By noon sun's tongue is hanging out
rocks sizzle, split and bake
a lizard frilled
a lizard grilled
birds uninvited guests

Angry wind bites into dusk
sandy teeth their imprint leave
bush melons flaunt
invite and taunt
proving too bitter to eat

But when parched hearts crack
desert flowers inspire hope
in harsh world living
solace giving
life is born from duress

17

Lessons learnt from my friends at Crossroads Disability Program

Soul Stirrings

The boy who walks around
with a guitar he can't play
exudes his love of music
and teaches me to absorb
every note I hear

The young woman with the
doll always in her arms
reveals her longing for the
child she will never have
and reminds me to cherish my children

The young man tightly clutching
a ball in his hands
perhaps remembers a time without a
wheelchair
and I am so grateful for every step I take

The smiling woman wearing
the iridescent pink hat
is shouting 'I'm here, please
don't ignore me'
and it's a privilege to share
her effervescence

The man who loves to
conduct the singing
standing with an empty music stand
lights up with enthusiasm
while my heart breaks

The girl with the plastic microphone
soundlessly moves lips
silently connecting to the dancing
and noise around her
grabbing precious moments
to be like everyone else

As I befriend and observe
it is profoundly clear
that no-one has a disabled
soul and I know
God is beaming as we dance
and laugh together

KNOWING GOD

To notice dew on the roses
to relax in the warmth of the sun
to be caressed by a cooling breeze
to watch sunsets when day is done

To forgive when friends desert you
to trust when all goes wrong
to have peace in the midst of sorrow
to be patient though the wait be long

To have inner strength when exhausted
to smile with a broken heart
to pray when your soul is so empty
to love when you think that you can't -
Is to know God

Raindrops trickling
green leaves glistening
geckos slithering
blessings on the way

Raindrops refreshing
nature redressing
her beauty extending
blessings on the way

Raindrops cleansing
man's faith strengthening
God is sending
blessings on the way

RAIN

DROPS

WHATEVER THE ANSWER

If the answer is yes
we rejoice
laugh for joy
so easy
to trust and be glad

If the answer is no
we panic
but He's there
to lead us
in better new ways

If the answer is wait
we rebel
hate delays
impatient
with His timing

Whatever the answer
He knows best
no mistakes
only love
surrounds His plan for all

PONDERING THE MYSTERY
OF UNANSWERED PRAYER

Norway at her best

Undeserved Jewels

Jewels
glistening, aglow
He drops to his children
below
not earned
but bestowed
from the Master's mine of treasures
to uplift and enrich
the souls of men

Sorrow

No-one sees the bleeding wound
no-one feels the pain
no-one understands the loss
no-one knows the strain -
no-one but Jesus

No-one can heal the hurt
no-one dry the tears
no-one fill the emptiness
no-one calm the fears -
no-one but Jesus

While working as a Funeral Director, Funeral Celebrant and currently as a Facilitator of a Grief and Loss Course, I long for others to be embraced by the One who truly understands suffering

Gift of dawn
strokes my eyes
glowing with anticipation
waiting in expectation
for my welcome

Gift of work
invades my day
needing my participation
rewarding with stimulation
as I increase

Gift of friends
recharges my soul
sharing in affirmation
healing from confrontation -
breath of new hope

Gift of sleep
envelops my mind
soothing with relaxation
nurturing by restoration -
it's good to be alive

GRA

TITUDE

Empty Nest

Empty nest
screams
all are gone
tears flow
with deep pain of loss

Empty nest
reminds
of love and warmth
the past
is revisited in your heart

Empty nest
whispers
job well done
watch now
their strengthened wings in flight

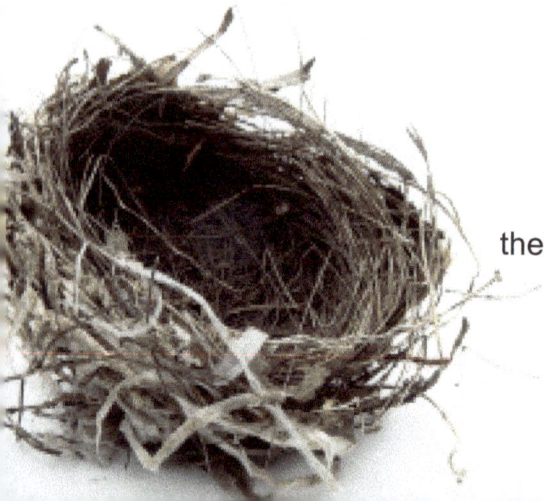

THE GREAT CREATOR

Who put the stripes on the zebra
who put the buzz in the bee
who put the frog in the tadpole -
the God who made you and me

Who put the seeds in the apple
who put the sap in the tree
who put the smell in carnations -
the God who made you and me

Who put the red in the sunset
who gave me two eyes to see
Who made the heart to love beauty -
the God who made you and me

FIRST PUBLISHED 1983 IN
FORTESQUE AND FRIENDS,
AN ILLUSTRATED VOLUME
OF CHILDREN'S POEMS,
MY FIRST BOOK, NOW
OUT OF PRINT

FRACTURED

Fractured -
emotions
families
friends
raw and sore
screaming for help

Fractured -
skilful hands
must find
and bind
frayed ends
together

Fractured -
not fatal
if we
invite
the soothing touch
of the Divine Healer

Spirit of Christmas

Spirit of Christmas
as seen by man
comes in a bottle
thoughts to throttle
no understanding
of why it began

Spirit of Christmas
brings strain and stress
too tired from rushing
too full from stuffing
empty hearts cry for
meaning in the mess

Spirit of Christmas
as seen by God
shows love in a stable
love that enables
mankind to live
grow and belong

Spirit of Christmas
draws us aside
to touch, see and feel
the meaning so real
and the heart of God
full and opened wide

Let's decide this year to lock out the thieves of
Christmas and invite in forgiveness and love.
'Let there be peace on earth and let it begin in me.'
(Jill Jackson)

ROLLED AWAY

The stone was rolled away
from my fluctuating faith
my stress
my mess
rolls it back in place.
The rock
can still block
access to Him.

The stone was rolled away
from my dark place
from tears
from fears.
I'll flee the clutching shadows
with Your power
me endow.
Let miracle dawn daily in my heart.

The stone was rolled away
help me run boldly into the Sunshine.

WANDERING THROUGH THE
GROUNDS OF A BEAUTIFUL
COUNTRY RETREAT AT EASTER
2012 DURING A TOUGH FAMILY
TIME, ENABLED ME TO REFOCUS
ON WHERE MY HELP COMES FROM

ETERNITY

Robbed of health and strength for living
independence and dignity past
robbed of some who friendship promised
shattered body, aching heart

Yet over painful questions great
shimmering rainbows of hope are poised
in my spirit there's no disease
faith and trust won't be destroyed

With each loss has come added gain
as His innocent suffering is mine
revealing treasures in darkness
riches within being mined

Lying in brokenness I wait
from cruel rejection never free
but the balm of God's love is renewing
till I run into eternity

THE FAITH OF THIS INCREDIBLE WOMAN,
IN HOSPITAL DYING OF AIDS CONTRACTED
THROUGH CONTAMINATED BLOOD,
BROUGHT ME TO TEARS AND COMPELLED
ME TO RECORD HER THOUGHTS

New Life

Smooth, brown earth
lying undisturbed
rudely wakens
to noise
of tortuous plough

Latent sod
is tossed and torn
scattered
by force
greater than itself

Fertile earth senses
it's not destroyed,
for new life
is being placed
in brokenness

Earth smiles again;
untouched
it is useless -
broken,
it bears fruit

ACCEPTED

OUR GRIEF JOURNEYS TAKE US ON A LONG WINDING
ROAD WITH STEEP HILLS AND VALLEYS BUT AS
LONG AS WE DON'T STOP WALKING, ACCEPTANCE
WILL EVENTUALLY BE OUR DESTINATION

ACCEPTANCE

In the turmoil
in the mess
in despair's dark pit
anger rages
panic cages
as entrapped you sit

Thoughts racing
body tense
emotional pain cuts deep
heart breaks
soul aches
in fear you weep

In the silence
in the void
finally you dare to hope
struggle lessens
patience beckons
God gives strength to cope

In the blackness
tiny beams of
light and love caress
new normal revealed
you emerge more real
changing and finding rest

COMO BRIDGE

Morning magic shimmers
as unseeing train proceeds
commuters asleep
miss beauty deep
but nature is all-embracing
in ten seconds over Como Bridge

Morning mist disguises
transforms into vision grey
not seeing yet aware
purpose still there -
sun penetrates fogs of life
recognised over Como Bridge

Morning miracle mirrors
a message to observant hearts
select peace and life
reflect love not strife
so others may read us
like vista over Como Bridge

FOR MANY YEARS I TRAVELLED TO WORK
IN SYDNEY BY TRAIN AND WAS AMAZED
THAT SO MANY PEOPLE MISSED THE MAGIC
AND CHANGING HUES IN THE DAILY
TEN SECONDS OVER COMO BRIDGE

FOR THOSE STRUGGLING WITH THE ONGOING
BATTLE OF MENTAL ILLNESS, ACCEPTING
THE CONDITION AND ACCEPTING HELP CAN
MAKE A HUGE DIFFERENCE TO LIFE. THIS
MAN FOUND SOLACE IN WATER AND BOATS

Greek Island of Corfu

His Goal

Sent to hospital not knowing why
made to take pills that flatten the highs
forced to stay in when he
wants to stay out
treatment given often causes him doubt

Mental illness bizarre and cruel
as he fights himself in a constant duel
life is controlled by others it seems
and stigma remains – will
he ever be free?

So many losses, so little rest
peace is elusive when he's depressed
so easy for us, is struggle for him –
do we see his pain as he
attempts to just live?

Please don't avoid him,
you've nothing to fear
like us he simply longs to be near

his shredded dreams have
been ripped apart
he can't bear it if we also
stomp on his heart

When his mind is in torment
we don't understand
that rejection and loneliness
take upper hand
so let's wait and remember
that God loves him still
his soul is intact, there's a plan to fulfil

He can't do it alone but
tries hard to cope
to accept who he is despite
limited scope
not many are perfect, not
many are whole
but he's worth something –
can he discover that goal?

CELEBRATION

She's here but not here
she's with me but not with me
she's awake but not aware
occasionally I look up to see
mum smiling at me
a silent smile, a wordless smile
a smile of love that rips my heart

Now she's not here
but still with me
she's awake in God's arms
occasionally I look up to see
mum smiling at me
a glowing smile, a knowing smile
a radiant smile that explodes my heart

MY MOTHER MARJORIE WAS MY
INSPIRATION. I CHOOSE TO REMEMBER
HER AS YOUNG AND VIBRANT, NOT
WITH DEMENTIA THAT CLAIMED
THE LAST 10 YEARS OF HER LIFE

FOR MARJORIE

Always there for family and friends
kind, generous and warm
mum was our rock
nothing could block
her love through every storm

Brave in disappointment
strong when setbacks came
persevering with grace
nothing too hard to face
this legacy with us remains

At her touch flowers grew
as did all those she loved
Her life's now with God
but her fragrance lives on
a gift to our hearts from above

BEST FRIEND

Never too busy
never too tired
always on duty
always by her side

Every sob brought him close
placing paw in her lap
every tear brought compassion
giving love in fur wrapped

How much we can learn
from our furry friends
as in silence they give
 and keep giving again

When my daughter's partner died suddenly in 2017, Bodhi, her border collie, was her comfort through many heart-breaking days and nights

Rules for Grandparents

If they won't eat fruit
dip it in chocolate

Sausages and sauce with
chips and sauce
is a perfectly balanced meal

If you make square sandwiches
on a triangle day
RUN FOR THE HILLS

When feeding the birds, break
the bread yourself -
we almost choked 10 ducks on the lake

Don't take child and scooter for a walk
as you'll end up carrying both home

When they spill popcorn at
movies, push under seat -
that's why it's dark in there

When at pool with diving sticks,
kids dive, you throw –
not the other way round

Kids are messy, noisy, exhausting
but their love, hugs and
kisses make our day

When they leave, visit physiotherapist
then impatiently wait to do it all again

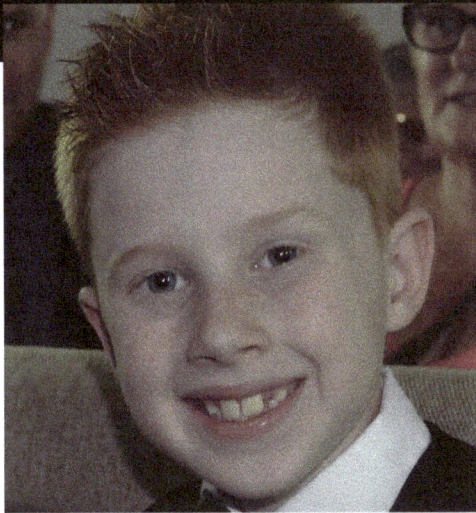

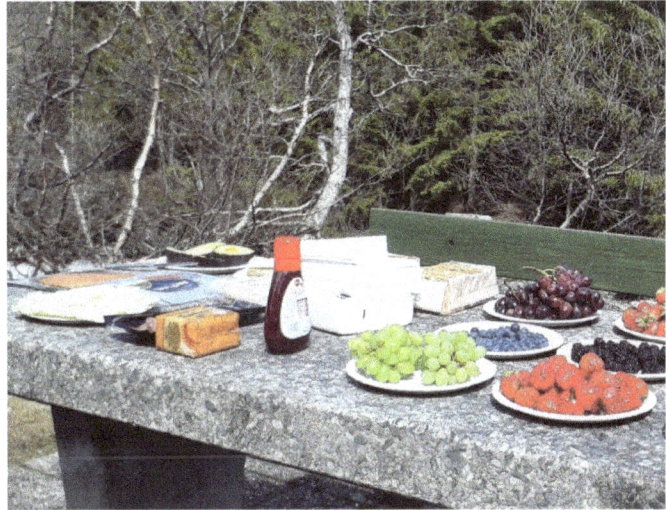

Whatever the shape or colour, just eat it !!!

Renewal

Gone hidden pain and anger
gone chill fear and dread
gone the tears of heartbreak
gone ugly blame – all have fled
darkness fierce
now is pierced

Come new strength and acceptance
come warm dreams replacing strife
come rich power of forgiving love
come discovery of sight and light
sunshine's rays
touch each day

THIS IS MY PRAYER FOR ALL SHATTERED,
DYSFUNCTIONAL FAMILIES, THAT THEY
WILL SEE HEALING OF RELATIONSHIPS
AND FORGIVENESS

Mossman Gorge, North Queensland

DEEP ROOTS

Buffeted by wind
weak tree
snaps
branches flap -
shallow roots

Buffeted by wind
strong tree
stands
strengthens bands -
deep roots

Buffeted by wind
lives can
break
or bend to take
life's storms

Buffeted by wind
deepens
faith
when roots are firmly
embedded in Him

HELD

She said

too numb to feel
too tired to care
nothing to fight with
reduced and bare
stripped of purpose
stripped of control
nothing but darkness
surrounding my soul

God says

I'm in the darkness
I'm holding your life
creating beauty and strength
and light in your night
like fragile blossoms
in the wind still intact
feel the warmth of my love
and let us welcome you back

OFFERING ENCOURAGEMENT
TO A FRIEND IN HOSPITAL
WHO WAS FEELING THE
STIGMA OF MENTAL ILLNESS

After winter comes spring

Eleven u-bends in a coach in Norway

ROAD OF LIFE

Do we shuffle
in our slippers
or stride
in shoes
with strength?

Do potholes
mar our progress
or challenge
advance
each day?

Does His presence
on the journey
make all
the ruts
worthwhile?

On the road that
winds before us
simply
follow His
footprints

LET THE MIRACLE OF THE GRUB'S
TRANSFORMATION INTO BEAUTIFUL BUTTERFLY
RESONATE IN YOUR CIRCUMSTANCES

NOTHING TOO HARD

I said

too weak to overcome

too burdened to rest

too hurt to forgive

too tired to love

He says

no more than you can bear

no load I can't lighten

no wound I can't heal

no hope I can't renew

Smiles of Love

She came towards me with a beaming smile
always wanting to connect
so innocent, so honest, so real
reaching out to those she can trust

He called my name in his loud, boisterous way
shuffled straight at me for a hug
although not allowed, he isn't aware
it's what friends do, isn't it?

Some social graces they don't understand
but if I'm sad, they're very discerning
more alert to my feelings than those who should see
reading so clearly, in touch with me

Our Choice

Biting like an icy wind
cold as frostbite
wounding like a sword
stripped as a bare winter tree -
criticism

Soothing like a cool breeze
warm as sunshine
healing like a balm
enveloping with love -
encouragement

INJUSTICE

Like disposables
we are tossed aside
hurting and raw
bruised and sore
absent love
cuts to the core

Like welcoming light
God draws us close
soothing and warm
becoming less torn
healing love
is hope reborn

Separation of divorce and domestic violence cuts deep

Lake Louise, Canada

R.I.P.

Death of a friend
like a raw, open wound
painful
disdainful
emotions strewn

Confusion and hurt
like eclipse of the sun
stumbling
and fumbling
alone on the run

Rest in peace comes
to the living in time
healing
revealing
scar to remind

Life is renewed
like the flowers in spring
cleaving
believing
to God we cling

Butchart Gardens, Vancouver Island

THE RAINBOW

Beaten, tired, discouraged

I can't go on like this

my caring service questioned

hurt and angry, perhaps I'll quit

overburdened is my heart

how many more poisoned darts?

God answered with a rainbow

beautiful, instant and mine

precious reminder that always

He knows, sees and hears my cries-

caressed by healing colours soft

I am loved, it's worth the cost

If we allow it, discouragement will paralyse

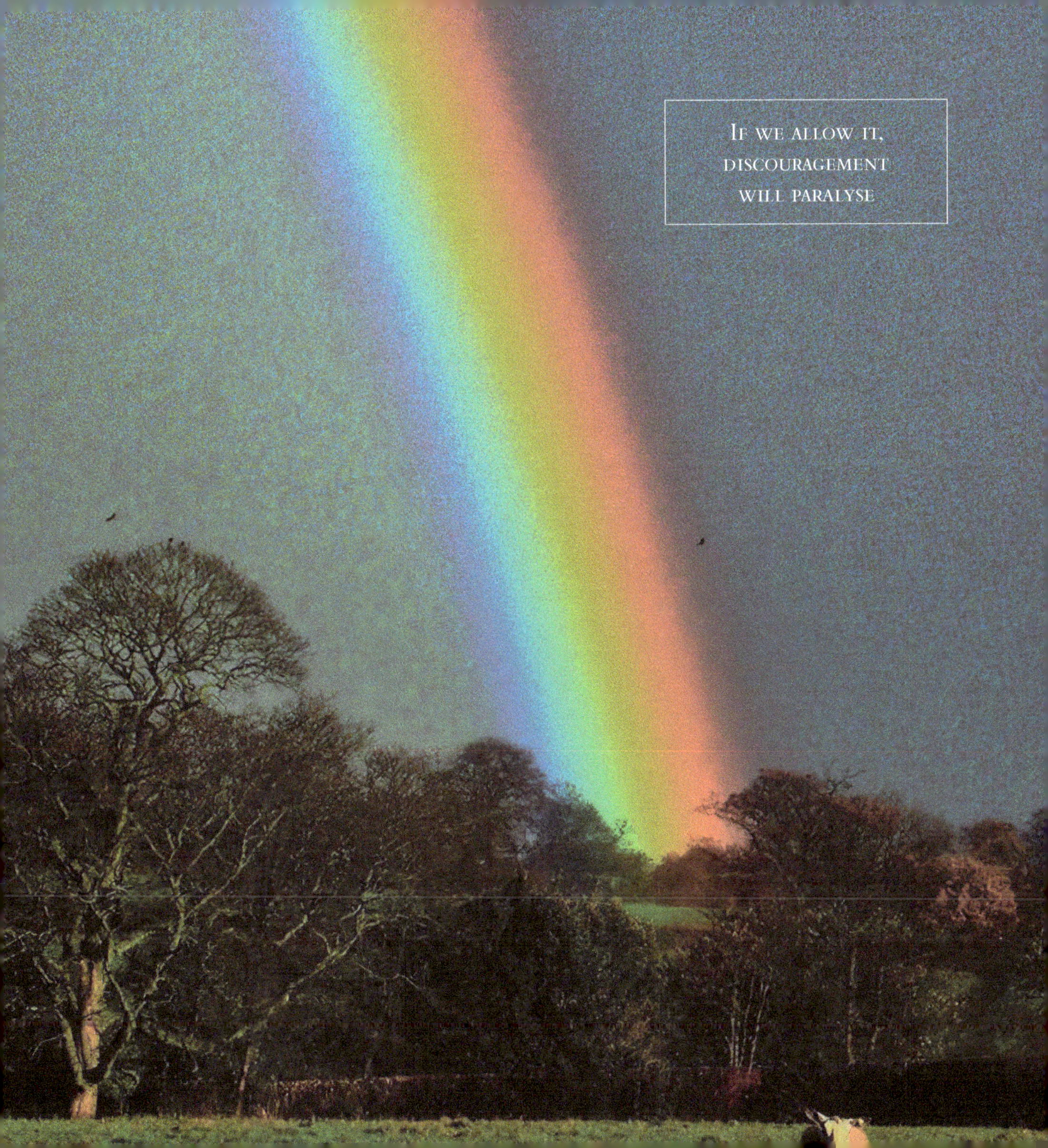

LOVE

Love not nails that held Him

love not thorns
that caused His brow to bleed

love not sword that pierced His side

love not hate
that brought about His death

love not wood that was His cross

Heart's Desire

Years pass
faith grows
but wonders why
heart's desire
is
withheld

Time and
love are
in my hands
forgotten never
says
the Lord

Heart's desire
will be
bestowed
when it will bless
you
the most

LIFE IS NOT A FAIRY TALE BUT
GOD SEES THE REAL PICTURE
AND BLESSES US AT JUST
THE RIGHT TIME

ENOUGH

When storms overtake us
frighten and wake us
God understands
and holds our hand

When illness finds us
scares and binds us
God understands
and holds our hand

When questions confuse us
and answers elude us
God understands
and holds our hand

When to trust is so tough
his love is enough
God understands
and holds our hand

WRITTEN FOR A FRIEND WHILE
RECOVERING FROM A STROKE

TODAY

Today the sun caresses me
daffodils warmly smile
smell of warm earth
chatter of birds
makes life worthwhile

Today the pain has lessened
able to clearly think
plan for tomorrow
complete simple tasks
of life's elixir drink

Today I can ring a friend
whose struggles are also tough
sharing each small step
and reality that knows
one day has to be enough

Today is a new, personal gift
tomorrow remains unknown
one day at a time
is all I need
this day I'll live and own

DAWN OF DISASTER

New year dawned
fresh and untouched
waiting events to own
hopes, dreams, plans
expectations of change
poised on the edge of unknown

Shroud of smoke
city ringed with flames
firestorms exploded en masse
hot, searing wind
devastation unleashed
heartbreak and tears mixed with ash

Fury of fire
out of control
blackened homes and hearts
scared children
stood in eerie glow –
how do you make a new start?

Burning throats
and burning trees
burning anger at the loss
confusion and shock
chilling in the heat
numbed minds assessing the cost

Beauty from ashes
is a promise from God
trust in midst of fierce pain
can true praise
ever come from despair
as you fight your faith to retain?

CONVERSATION WITH FRIEND AFTER
LOSING HOME AND POSSESSIONS IN
SYDNEY FIRES, JANUARY 1994

SIGNED BY GOD

His hand all around us
astounds and reveals
majesty, power
message clear.
Can we recognise
God's signature?

His hand on our hearts
burns words for life
into living truth
etched with love.
Do we reveal
God's signature?

Norway begins to thaw

Banff, Canada

FIRST PUBLISHED 1983 IN
FORTESQUE AND FRIENDS,
AN ILLUSTRATED VOLUME OF CHILDREN'S
POEMS, MY FIRST BOOK, NOW OUT OF PRINT

THE PROBLEM WITH BIRDS

I love the way the kookaburras laugh
I love the sparrows hopping on the path
I love cockatoos screeching before dark
but why don't birds wear nappies?

I love the emus with their great big feet
I love the pelicans with funny beaks
I love small canaries that sing so sweet
but why don't birds wear nappies?

God made every bird - some big and some small
it would be so silly to dress them all
for we'd never see soft feathers which fall -
that's why birds don't wear nappies

THESE HANDS

We'd only just met
but she hugged me
a hug that cried help
a hug that felt lonely
'like me' her plea

She is ill and scared
in emotional pain
is hospital haven?
is hospital hell?
will she ever be well again?

I felt her trembling
heard her silent scream
my touch said 'I'm here'
my touch whispered I care
don't give up your dreams

No words were spoken
true self searching to find
God was shouting 'I love you'
God was showing life's for you too
these hands that hold you are Mine

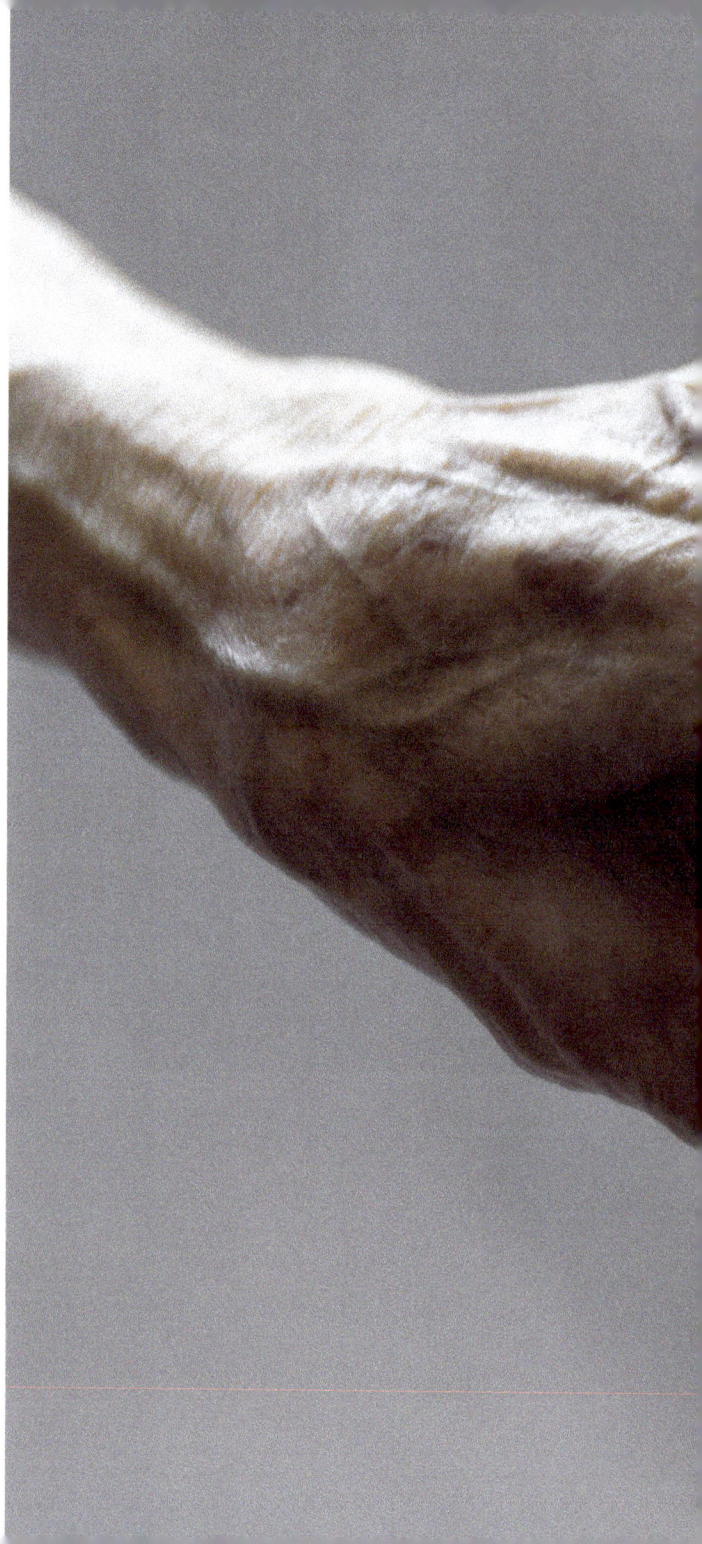

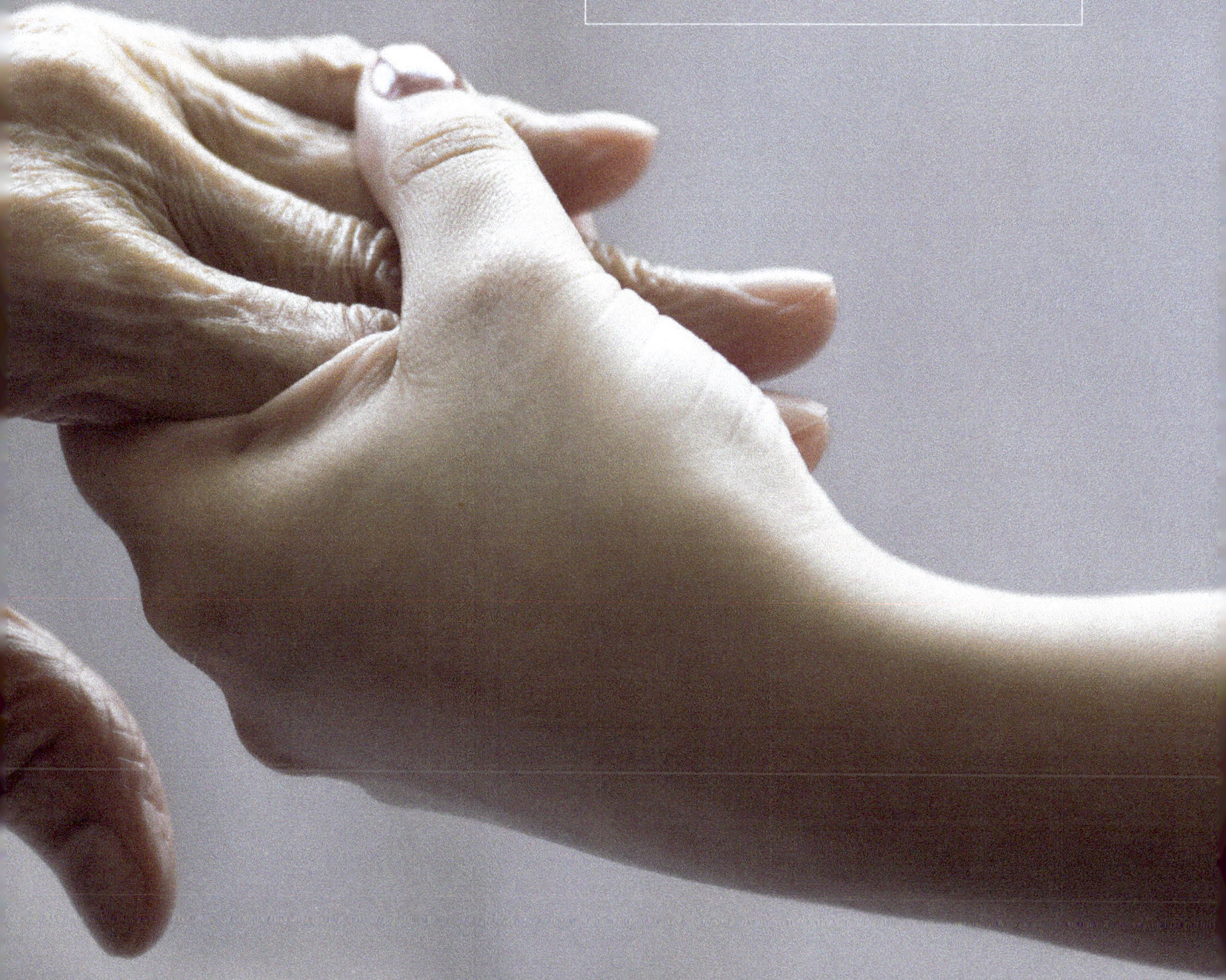

Sweden is known for its scenic lakes and forests

Choked

Sunset on the lake
seems calm, almost serene
but marring
the surface -
weeds

Choking weeds, clinging weeds,
sapping strength and life
ever spreading
and spoiling
all

What weeds are hidden
behind our false facade?
Dig out and let
true beauty
emerge

Two Trees

Two trees touching
branches entwined-
giving strength
when winds start
when heat blasts

One tree torn down
leaving glaring gap-
now misshapen
exposing spaces
vulnerable places

Remaining tree waits
regrowth begins-
offering shelter and shade
as life refuels
as hope renews

Death separates
love restores-
God and others
will help remake
will help reshape

THIS ANALOGY RESONATES
WITH MANY WHO HAVE LOST
THEIR LIFE PARTNER

DIVINE DANCE

Musician sang and played Elvis
group stomped and yelled and clapped
ear shattering and fast
all having a blast
in universal music wrapped

Musician hot and sweating changed pace
sang *How Great Thou Art* in slow beat
no direction was given
silence fell as if bidden
gently swaying, arms high, stilled feet

I saw worship and peace
I saw divine dance
I saw God
and felt goose bumps on my soul

I GAIN FAR MORE FROM MY WEEKLY
VOLUNTEERING AT CROSSROADS
DISABILITY PROGRAM THAN I GIVE.
FOR ME IT IS ALWAYS SOUL THERAPY

North Stradbroke Island, Queensland

SEASCAPE

Sight, sound and smell of sea
captivate me

Cool, clear, crystal spray
refreshes me

Screeching, scavenging seagulls
amuse me

Presence, power and plan of Creator
humble me

How many moods has the ocean?
I have lived close to the ocean
all my life and am still finding
more. Here it is frolicking

99

SPLINTERS

In love you dig out that splinter
and cause the tears to flow
in love you remove the intruder
and sometimes anger sow

In love you dig out that splinter
despite the pleas of 'sore'
in love the invader must leave
even when you hurt more

In love there is a cost to bear –
how willingly we pay
in love God removes our splinters
if we let Him have His way

MASKED

Behind the mask
complete the task
and never ask
who am I?

Behind the mask
in safety bask
no depth that lasts -
who am I?

Remove the mask
on Him all cast
deal with the past
who am I?

Remove the mask
show Him so vast
no-one will ask
who am I?

TO BE UNMASKED MAKES
US MORE VULNERABLE
BUT IT'S WORTH IT
TO BE REAL AND AT PEACE
WITH OURSELVES

NEW DIRECTION

Seagull flailing
seagull failing
against the wind

Seagull tiring
seagull striving
against the wind

Slowly turning
strength returning
helped by wind

Like the gull
when all seems lost –
change direction

WITHOUT HIM

Without knowing I will trust
without understanding I will wait
without God there is no meaning
without Him my soul is bare

without fear I'll face each day
without regret I'll obey His voice
without God no future waits
without Him my heart won't care

without His love life's incomplete
without forgiveness I'm in chains
without God I'm fractured still
without Him my peace can't dare

GOD'S CANVAS

Seasonal changes
here to enrich
hues light and dark
hues soft and hard
sometimes so still
sometimes cascading

Petals and leaves
uniquely designed
no colour the same
no smell lost in rain
sometimes in bud
sometimes full flowering

God's colour scheme
implodes in our hearts
not a black and white vista
not a black and white world
sometimes we are blind
sometimes appreciating

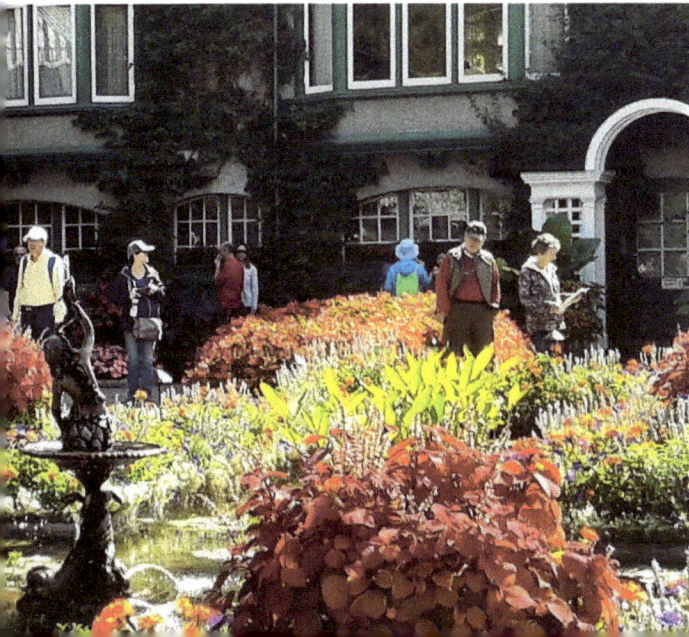

ENDORSEMENTS

Dawn of Hope, Kept by Love, Shaped

Just finished reading *Dawn of Hope* and loved it! It tugged on the heart strings while shedding light on important life struggles, all the while providing comic relief and a valuable insight into my favourite line of work. A great read. AMY

You write well, with great clarity, your characters are likable and the story pulls the reader along. Your experience in your fields is impressive and I admire the way you've translated all that wisdom into a novella that's insightful and charming at the same time.   RD

Having been a Funeral Celebrant and Hospital Chaplain for many years myself, I identified completely with the characters and situations you wrote about. Couldn't put the books down. Who says men don't read fiction? Keep writing!   DON

Kept by Love was funny, sad, full of practical information about wills, funerals, and an insight into mental health. At the same time a beautiful story full of faith and love with a happy ending. ELIZABETH

A very good read. Great learning curve and impactful. First two pages had me hooked. Shows a unique understanding of people struggling with life. CM

Beautifully written, captivating stories of love and understanding. ANNE

Read *Shaped* in one night. Couldn't put it down. What a beautiful, sad, inspiring story. Congratulations on everything you have achieved and become. Thank you for sharing your story with me and the world. RH

Kaye's book *Shaped* is an insightful, touching autobiography. It was a genuine privilege to share in her emotional and spiritual journey. Kaye's account of early family life and the subsequent effects on all involved is both heart breaking and heart warming. Central to the book is her willingness to be shaped and formed by the "Master Potter." Thank you Kaye MELINDA

Kaye Hollings writes with penetrating honesty. In managing to be so open about her "non-relationship" to her grandmother and the pain that this "thorn in her life" brought, she helps all of us to courageously face our life's hurdles. REV JOHN GILES

Shaped is an inspiring true story. The book is a tapestry where we see loose ends and a bit of a mess on one side and on the flip side the threads of Kaye's love and trust in her Creator and quirky sense of humour make a beautiful picture.

An inspirational read. JANINE

Such vulnerability is shown in this book which only a mature and honest woman like Kaye can do. Thanks Kaye. We can all learn much from this as you've shown us through your struggles, which may be similar to many of our own, the path to wholeness and maturity. SUE

Your book *Shaped* is wonderful and loved by everyone who reads it. Great clarity and insight. PAUL

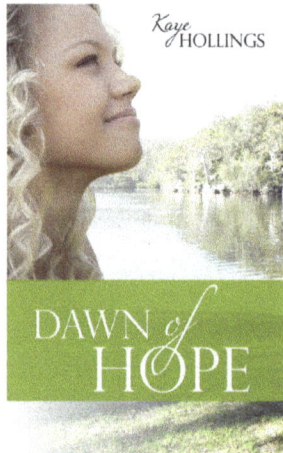

DAWN OF HOPE

Book 1

ISBN: 978-0-9875839-0-1

Publisher: arkhousepress.com

From hospital to hope,
from brokenness to wholeness–
could it happen for her?

In Sydney, Australia, in the 21st century, it is still difficult to be different. Despite anti-discrimination and equal opportunity laws, there are social stigmas firmly in place and Toni is fighting for survival. Will her secret have to remain hidden forever?

Low self-esteem and loneliness are her first obstacles, and coming to terms with her father's death unpacks some surprising revelations.

Working with animals is more rewarding than competing with humans and throwing herself into her job provides humor and light relief in her world of struggle and misunderstanding.

But Toni soon realizes she wants more from life. She wants love, an enduring relationship and a meaningful future. As she explores faith and loss, self-acceptance and purpose, she takes us on a heart-warming journey through sadness and doubt, mirth and elation, to unknown possibilities.

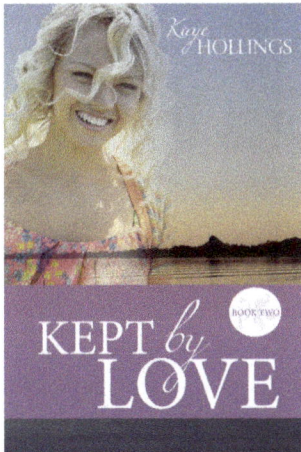

KEPT BY LOVE
Book 2
ISBN: 978-0-9923452-6-6
Publisher: arkhousepress.com

As her perfect world begins to crumble, can she find strength to cope with dashed hopes and shattered emotions?

To accept yourself, like what you see, and acknowledge that others like what they see, had been a long process for Toni. For over a year she'd been basking in the warmth of being married to the man of her dreams and working in a new career she loved, but vulnerability and uncertainty were never far from the surface.

She couldn't know that someone unexpected would enter her life, revealing hidden secrets from the past and neither was she prepared for established norms to irrevocably change and be tested.

Being married meant learning to communicate at a deeper level, sharing plans and goals, and she begins to question life and belief. What did she have to contribute? How do you move forward during the tough times?

As we journey with Toni again, we share her laughter and tears as she tries to balance doubt and faith, loss and blessing, sadness and joy. Will she lose herself in the fight to survive or discover what really matters in life?

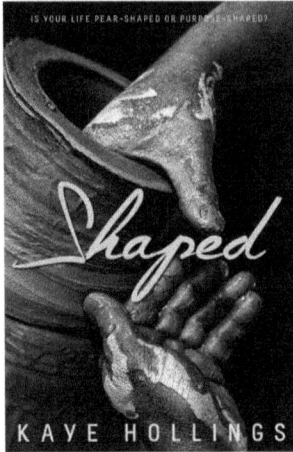

SHAPED

ISBN: 978-0-6481016-7-3
Publisher: arkhousepress.com

What shape is your soul?
Who or what is shaping you now?

Once upon a time there was a young girl living with a mentally ill grandmother, with no self-esteem, no confidence, no purpose, and with a fierce dislike of psychiatric wards.

Through it all she became a writer, a mental health chaplain and then a funeral director after a long, winding but exciting journey.

That woman is Kaye Hollings. In her book, Shaped, she tells her story of being raw clay: moulded, fired in the kiln of life, reworked, re-fired, fashioned and glazed.

Shaped retraces her steps, helping you to potentially discover your own revealed path, emerge from life's confusing maze, and find yourself in the safe hands of the Divine Potter.

www.ingramcontent.com/pod-product-compliance
Lightning Source LLC
Chambersburg PA
CBHW040848100426
42813CB00015B/2747